Teach the Children the

The Family
A Proclamation to the World

Simplified meaning for children
by Jeanne W. Anderson

Illustrated by Amy L. Hintze

Good Mountain Home Publishing

To order additional copies of this book email:
goodmountainhome@gmail.com

or write to:
 671 Ridge Dr.
Alpine, UT 84004

This book is lovingly dedicated to
President Gordon B. Hinckley and to his wife, Sister Marjorie P. Hinckley
for the marvelous example they set of a loving marriage and a strong family.

Oh, how I miss them!

The last sentence of *The Family, a Proclamation to the World* states,
"We call upon responsible citizens and officers of government everywhere to promote those measures designed to maintain
and strengthen the family as the fundamental unit of society."

Through the words and illustrations of this book, I am striving to do my part to promote, maintain, and strengthen the family.
I hope this book will be a means to help all of you to teach the children in your life these important, God-given principles.

100% of the net profits of this book will be donated to the General Missionary Fund of the
Church of Jesus Christ of Latter-day Saints.

Special thanks to:
My friend Amy Hintze for her thoughtful, beautiful illustrations,
my son Ryan for his excellent book design, and to
my husband Steve for his love and support in this endeavor.

On September 23, 1995, at the tabernacle of the Church of Jesus Christ of Latter-day Saints in Salt Lake City, Utah, President Gordon B. Hinckley gave an important message to the world. President Hinckley was the prophet on the earth at that time. A prophet communicates with God and is His special messenger on the earth. This very important message was titled, *The Family, a Proclamation to the World*.

The proclamation tells us that "marriage between a man and a woman is ordained of God and that the family is central to the Creator's plan for the eternal destiny of his children." This means that God wants marriage to only be between a man and a woman. God, our creator, wants all of us to be part of a family for eternity. That means forever!

All of us are a spirit son or daughter of our Heavenly Parents. We were created in their image. Men look like our Heavenly Father, and women look like our Heavenly Mother. "Gender is an essential characteristic of our premortal, mortal, and eternal identity and purpose." This means that boys will always be males and that girls will always be females. No one can change that!

$\mathcal{W}$e all lived in Heaven before we were born on the earth. We worshiped our Heavenly Father. We accepted God's plan that we would come to earth to "obtain a physical body and gain earthly experience to progress towards perfection." We have a divine destiny or a God-given blessing to have eternal life. This means we will be able to live forever with Heavenly Father and Jesus.

$\mathcal{B}$ecause of sacred ordinances and covenants or promises made in holy temples, we can also be together as a family in Heaven. God's plan of happiness says that even when our loved ones die, we can be with them again!

The first people on the earth were Adam and Eve. God commanded them to multiply and replenish the earth. This means that they should have children. God still wants men and women who are lawfully married to have children. The sanctity or sacredness of life is important in God's eternal plan.

*P*arents need to love and care for each of their children. They should do their best to provide for their children's physical needs with a warm home, food, and clothing. Parents should also provide for the spiritual needs of their children by teaching them the commandments of God, to love and serve others, and to obey the laws of their country.

"The family is ordained of God. Marriage between a man and a woman is essential to His eternal plan." Children have the right to be reared by a father and a mother who are completely loyal to each other.

"*Happiness in family life is most likely to be achieved when founded upon the teachings of the Lord Jesus Christ.*"

"*S*uccessful marriages and families are established and maintained on the principles of faith, prayer, and repentance...

forgiveness, respect, love, and compassion...

work and wholesome recreational activities."

$\mathscr{B}$y God's design, "fathers are to preside over their families in love and righteousness and are responsible to provide the necessities of life and protection for their families."

"*M*others are primarily responsible for the nurture of their children." Fathers and mothers should help each other as equal partners. If a mom or dad gets hurt or dies, or there are other problems, then changes might have to be made. Our extended family of grandparents, aunts and uncles should give us help when needed.

Sad things will happen to those people who don't obey the commandments of God. We all need to help "maintain and strengthen the family as the fundamental unit of society." We need to teach the family proclamation to all the people in the world!

Our family loves to have a weekly Family Home Evening.
Here is a suggested format:

Welcome

Opening Song: "Families Can Be Together Forever"
Church of Jesus Christ of Latter-day Saints, Children's Song Book, pg. 188

Opening Prayer

Scripture: Recited by the family, Doctrine and Covenants, Section 88:119

Lesson: Read and discuss *The Family, a Proclamation to the World* from the Church of Jesus Christ of Latter-day Saints. (This book will be helpful to younger children. Explain that the pictures of the children in Heaven are symbolic of our pre-earth life.)

Closing Song: "Teach Me to Walk in the Light"
Church of Jesus Christ of Latter-day Saints, Children's Song Book, pg. 177

Closing Prayer

Game: Indoor balloon volleyball is fun. Clear a space in your family room. Tie a rope about 4 feet high across the middle of the room connected to a chair on each side. Divide the family in half and have them sit on the floor on each side of the rope. Blow up a balloon. Players can serve the ball (balloon) with their hand, but after the serve, they can only use their feet to kick the ball over the rope. The rules are the same as volleyball except players use their feet!

Refreshments and Family Calendar Time: While eating refreshments, review your family calendar to correlate activities for the week with each other. This is especially important as children get older.

Lemon Bars are one of our very favorite F.H.E. treats. This recipe is for the best lemon bars ever!

LUSCIOUS LEMON BARS

Crust:
1 Cup soft butter
½ Cup sugar
2 Cups flour
Dash salt
Preheat oven to 350 degrees. Combine the above ingredients and mix well. Press the dough into a 9" X 13" baking pan. Bake for 15 minutes until lightly browned. Remove from the oven and let cool.

Filling:
4 eggs beaten
2 Cups sugar
¼ Cup flour
6 Tablespoons lemon juice
Beat the eggs. Add in the flour, sugar, and lemon juice. Pour this mixture onto the slightly cooled crust. Bake at 350 degrees for 25 minutes or until set. Cool and then sprinkle with powdered sugar. Makes 24 bars.

About the Author

Jeanne and her husband, Steve, currently reside in Alpine, Utah. They are the parents of five boys; thus, they have served as Boy Scout Leaders for over 20 years. Their family has grown as they now have five beautiful daughters that have married into the family. At the time of this writing, they have ten darling grandchildren! Jeanne has a Bachelor's Degree from Brigham Young University in Social Work. She loves gardening, all sports, being in the mountains, and writing stories for children. She is a 25 year volunteer with the Festival of Trees, a charity to help needy children at Primary Children's Hospital. If you would like to reach Jeanne or to order additional copies of this book, please contact her at goodmountainhome@gmail.com. She would love to hear from you!

About the Illustrator

Amy Hintze graduated from Brigham Young University with a Bachelor of Fine Arts degree in Illustration. In addition to drawing and painting for books and magazines, Amy is pursuing a degree in motherhood, with three adorable boys and two adorable girls. She has also enjoyed illustrating the Mormon Tabernacle Choir's Music and the Spoken Word broadcast since 2007. In her nonexistent spare time she enjoys being in the outdoors, listening to music, yoga, teaching art, and spending quality time with her wonderfully supportive husband, Brian. Amy met Jeanne when her small family moved to Alpine in 2000. Amy currently resides with her rambunctious family in Lindon, Utah. See more of her artwork at amyhintzeart.blogspot.com

Teach the Children the Meaning of

The Family
A Proclamation to the World

In September of 1995, President Gordon B. Hinckley, the prophet on the earth, presented *The Family, a Proclamation to the World*. The purpose of this book is to teach the important messages of this proclamation in a simplified form for children. Beautiful illustrations accompany the text. This book is a resource to teach the children in a way that they will understand and remember the proclamation.

Good Mountain Home Publishing

65937151R00020

Made in the USA
Charleston, SC
05 January 2017